DREAM GIRL

Poems by
Clementine von Radics

For Alia,
Keep sharing

This was unlike the story
it was written to be.
I was riding its back
when it used to ride me.

—Joanna Newsom

Contents

For Barbara Jane,
Elizabeth,
and Eliza Jane

Dream Girl

Explaining Girlhood to a Boy
Who Has Never Been There

The thing is, no one looks at you and says *girl*.
They look at you and say *meal* and expect you
to say *Thank you*. You have to be a tidy feast.
A bloodless slaughter. You have to paint and
pluck and slather and starve. You have to break
your new, soft heart like breaking is your
birthright.

Maybe that is how it is for all girls. Maybe a girl
is born too much everything, and everything
she touches takes something from her. Maybe
to be a woman is to be a certain kind of hollow.
After all, for years I've seen the hollow in
everything. I pick up the house I grew up in
and throw it over my shoulder like it's nothing.
I learned early what this world wants of me.
I carve myself out and be that instead.

Sublimate

I wake up to my phone glowing

> u up still?

And in the dizzy smear of sleep,
I type

> Yes,
> come be bodies
> w me

I meet him at the door.
Lock fingers,
lead him to my bedroom.

I kiss him and say

> *I don't believe in truth anymore*

I kiss him and say

> *I am paralyzed by hope*

I kiss him and say

> *I'm gonna break you open*
> *and find the butterflies*
> *and beneath that the concrete*
> *and beneath that the rich dirt*

I kiss him and say

There is something in me cannot be healed.
There is something in me needs breaking open.

Sweet the Sound

When my fever hits 104, he puts me in the car
and drives me to the hospital. I tell him

> *There is a different kind of world out there*
> *and it is not called Heaven*
> *or any word they have taught me yet.*
>
> *In this place*
> *we have a language of untalking.*
> *None of us remembers*
> *what a scream sounds like.*
> *We have bodies, but they do not ache*
> *and this saves a wretch*
> *like me.*

In the blinking bright emergency room,
the nurse says *infection*. She says *It's all over you.*
I tell her

> *This world,*
> *I know we built it with our own hands*
> *and it is good.*

.

I tell her my smallest, truest hope:

> *May everything about this place*
> *remove me from myself.*

And this is the sickness talking,
the part of me so spoiled, rotting in the blood.
But so much of what I want
is to be less a person.

To be instead a word
too beautiful to fit inside my own
fevered, mumbling mouth.

> *When I imagine myself*
> *I am barely there.*

Truism

So I open up my body, whole
and spit-shined and eager
and inside there is nothing
but a mouth.

And the mouth says

You are not an easy person to love.

Curious, I reach into the mouth
and pull out its tongue.

And I make the tongue say it again
and again

You are not an easy person...
You are not an easy person to...

And it's so silly looking,
this little flip-flopping thing
in the palm of my hand.

So I show it to everyone.
To my friends, to the guy at 7-Eleven.
On the morning you leave
I hold it right up to your face.

So close you practically choke on it.
So close it practically becomes
your tongue.

And everyone
I show it to just looks at it
and laughs.

Of course, they say,
Of course this is true.

AN EXACT TRANSCRIPT
OF WHAT THAT MAN SHOUTED FROM HIS CAR
ON SEPTEMBER 25, 2015

Hey Girl, you tryna get catcalled? You wanna get fucked tonight? I keep going to bed alone, I want to change that. I'm reaching out, don't be mean. What about you? You'd love it. You'd live for it. I can change your life. Come on. You look really good today baby.

Why so angry? I'm just trying to be nice, Well fuck you too! Rude Bitch. You're a fucking rude ugly bitch. How about I get out of this car and hold you down and rape you? You want my cock in your mouth? I bet you'd be quiet then. You'd like that, huh?

Wait no no no no no no please stop screaming. I'm sorry. I'm sorry, ma'am. I'll go. I'm sorry. I messed up. I didn't mean it. Please calm down. Please stop yelling. I'm sorry. I'm sorry.

Thank you, thank you. I'm sorry. I'll go.

You know, you really did overreact.

I was just joking.

Dream Girl

He is constructing a god
out of my body
and I do not stop him.

This will make
a ghost of him
and me.

But tonight
he needs an altar
and I'm not here to be brave.

Courtney Love Prays to Oregon

This is the house they built me
and I'm gonna burn it down.

This is the river I crawled from
and I refuse to drown here.

And bless the strippers,
        and fuck the men.

And bless the fruit
        and fuck the farm.

And bless the daughter
        and fuck the family.

What is a home
if not the first place we learn to run from?

You've got to bite the hand
that starves you,
and doing so

praise the place that birthed you.

Birthed you Fucked Up.
Birthed you ugly, and interesting

and ready to scream.

Sick Girl in Support Group
Measures Her Luck in Increments

Round up in a cracking circle,
these women who share my sick
sit with warped, withered hands.

Their bodies, closing in on themselves,
look to me like the mouth of a bear trap
I have somehow escaped.

So in this sense I am lucky.

This is what luck means now:
to be less dead than everyone else in the room.

Look, how lucky

        I can walk.
        I can hold a job.
        I even smile a little.

When I Say I Don't Care
If I'm Beautiful

(But I do, and everyone
can tell, and its heart-
breaking)

What I mean is
all pretty ever got me
was down on my knees.

The Haus in North Portland

So we shove 7 people into a 3-bedroom house
and we do not call it *family* but
we call it something close.

Some word that is spoken loud
and rhymes with
the only place that does not open its jaws
to greet you.

This is our church of banjos,
our garden of collard greens and kale.
We are all dirt and belly laughs,
and look at us, we belong to this.
This crooked house,
we call it home.

One night in July we all take Molly
and I hold your hand and say
Look! We're bruised in all the same places
We laugh. We count our injuries,

and isn't this proof we've been saved?
Isn't this proof the world can come for you
with all its fists, and you can still find people
who share your soft.

And I wish the story could stop here.
I wish I didn't have to tell the next part.

How 3 days later
when I found the empty bottles,
I called the ambulance, broke
down your door, and was not fast
enough.

How the house still stood, but it felt
burned down and grief opened its jaws
to greet us and the dog growled at your door
for days.

We held a memorial for you in the garden.
All those collard greens and kale, everything
sang of your absence and never really
stopped singing.

Those of us who held or miss
your body, we are most of us happy now.
That doesn't make you less gone.
But what will?

2012

It was the fall we lost the cat, then soon after
lost the house. The fall of four jobs
and cold bus stops. A whole year spent
in the food stamp waiting room.
The year of the dog bite, the bad fever,
the bill collectors. The winter we had no heat
but each other's body, coincidentally, the winter
of cold bodies. The year of playing house.
Fucking in the kitchen and calling it freedom.
The year we had nothing, but it was our nothing,
and we earned it. The spring you burned your hand
on the stove and left a scar that long outlasted me.
The year you lied about the rent check,
and the good job, and the girl
who always looked at your mouth funny.
The year you said my heart was ugly; swollen with
devotion. That summer I came home from work
and found your keys on the counter, and half
the closet empty, and all the pictures of us still up
on the fridge. The night I called you again,
and again, and again and when you finally picked up
I said *I love you* when I meant something much more
specific. I should have said *Please don't leave me.*
I'm afraid to sleep alone.

Girlhood, As I Remember

I remember it all as a steam-colored dream,
the tender ritual of it, the smear of lipstick and
scrape of hairbrush. I held Sara's hand as she
painted my nails and the warmth of her felt
like a hot curling iron on the back of my neck.

We have a language of secrets, the girls like us.
We live inside a cloud of wonder. We practiced
kissing on the back of our hands and slept all
skinny limbs and heat and wanted something
we could not name.

Girl.
I want to change

your

angry
mouth
I bet you'd   like that, huh?

Vigil

This body wears crazy so well and so unlike a man.
Like well-sewn black lace and pink Moscato.

This body lit the votive candles above the bathtub
and forgot. They burned all night. The house stands.

Small miracle. This body fell asleep and woke up
with a kitchen knife in the bed. Again.

I am off somewhere in a swirl of blue silk, slow
and watching this body. My body.

I brought a knife to the gunfight. I am the knife.
I am all blade.

Anais Nin Prays to
Her Father's Piano

Praise be to you,
your keys and wire, his best voice,
for the only way I know to love a man
is to watch him alchemy failure
into music.

Sick Girl's Body
Threatens the Medicine

What do you know about a body
out to eat itself alive?

This body welcomes
every plague
like a dinner guest.

This body
knows pain
like an old lover.

This failing tangle of sinew
has now soured the meat.
Watch it eat away at anything left.

Let this body be a pestilence.
Let this mind be a ghost
or the famine that begat it.

When I Say I Hate Men

(But I don't. I have loved
so many good, soft hearts)

What I mean is
a few men
and a whole world built
to protect them

hurt me first,
and more, and in ways
I never even imagined.

It is easier to be angry
than afraid.

Nameless

You have to understand,
I was not a good home. Not yet.
I was barely more than a child.
I had always wanted a daughter.

In the parking lot of the clinic,
I cried until I could not breathe.
I never spoke of it. I always mourned.
I would do nothing different.

In Which a Girl's Body
Is Not a Flower or a Fruit

And she is not looked at
or swallowed.
And remains growing.
Rooted.

Wyoming

It wasn't just that I was leaving

(For the 2:40 bus.
For reasons that lived beneath the house.
Forever this time.)

It wasn't just that he said it

(It was the way he said it.
Standing in the doorway, his mouth
a thin clothesline. Asking for love
that had long dried up. His eyes
two bloodless sunsets,
warming nothing.)

It wasn't that I didn't say it back

(Couldn't soothe him
one last time. Wasn't that girl anymore.
Had a bus to catch. All night
to California.)

It was the way he knew
I would not say it

(Knew I hated him
for his weakness.
Knew I was not the girl
we had hoped I'd become.
Knew his heart disgusted me.

Knew
I had caught a butterfly
only to rub it with my hands
leave it winged
and without flight.)

Upon Hearing What He Did to You

I was sitting on my bed, drinking red wine.
I think *30 Rock* was on
in the background.

My friend told me what she overheard at work,
that you had scrambled out the window
in the middle of the night. You and he
had been together for years.
I only lasted six months.

My friend, she keeps talking and I imagine
I am dodging out of the path
of a speeding train.

I say *I guess it was only a matter of time* and I imagine
you wrapping your body around mine
like a bulletproof vest.

I say *I tried to warn her,* to love him is to learn
how to suck the poison from a snakebite. Only
when I say snakebite, I mean his mouth
and when I say poison, I mean also
his mouth.

I say *If you run in to her, tell her she can call me.*
Tell her I am pulling these fangs from my body
still, after all these hungry
empty years.

Girl

        keep screaming.

I am afraid

    of you.

And your

       good
          messed
          mouth.

That Night, I Learned the Truth of Him

But the next morning his eyes are still blue
like Wyoming sky, and I still love him.
And that is not permission

but it is complication.

So I spend the next year
in worship of those eyes.
His confessional mouth.

So my own body
becomes nothing but an altar
to his gentle hands.

And this makes a ghost
of him

and me.

What Brings Me Joy

You,
of course.
Always you.

You Are on the Floor Crying

And you
have been on the floor crying
for days.

And this is you being brave.

That is you
getting through this as best
you know how.

No one else gets to tell you

what your tough looks like.

Girl

keep screaming.

I am afraid

of you.

And your

good
messed
mouth.

In Defense
of My Behavior

He never broke my heart,
only turned it into a compass
that always points me
back to him.

Sylvia Plath Prays to the House above Her

House,
I know what they will say about me.
They will call me a crazy grave,
lost as my children.

I will not be forgiven for leaving this world
less politely than I should have.

I annihilate. I ash. I terrify.

House,
They will not understand the woman
who sees herself in me.
That will not undo her seeing.
We are all the same,
identical woman.

May she Lazarus from my words.

May she rise again

and again, and again.

Ways I Might Start the Last Poem
I Write for You

With thanks to Jack Gilbert

One:

> There was the night we got drunk
> on Olympias and Mountain Air
> and I told you the sound of your voice
> still chases me down on Sundays.

One:

> I don't know what to call the husk of us,
> The hollow carved out of fight
> and longing,
> But I think that word must sound
> like the passage of time.

One:

> You wouldn't believe the things
> that remind me of your hands.

One:

> I hate everyone with your name
> and this too is reluctant devotion.

One:

On those Sundays when I hear your voice,
I put on a Hank Williams record
and dance barefoot in my empty living room.
I wear my best lipstick. I flirt with
the stillness. I choose, for a few moments,
to forget that you really are gone.

One:

I know you still think of me
like I know there are horrible monsters
in the blackest parts of oceans.

I have been told enough times
I don't need proof that it's true.

When I Tried to Warn Her

I said, It's not that he[1]
was a bad guy,[2]
it's just that I can't breathe
when he's in the room[3]

---

[1] He will draw a chalk outline of a body
and you will fit inside it perfectly
and you still won't sense the killing.

[2] I cannot tell you how he hurt me
without fearing he'll do it again.

[3] And it was bad enough
when his mouth did them the first time.
They come out of me again and I won't survive.
I know what they do to girls like me.
I know how they forgive men like him.

Girl

keep screaming.

I am afraid

of you.

And your

good
messed
mouth.

The Fidelity of the Fourth Step

When the Boy from All the Old Poems
sends you a letter saying

I've been clean for 6 months now,
and I want to apologize for everything
my hands did back then.

Strangely,
it will not feel like healing.
Even if it is true. Even if
this is the kindest thing that boy
has done for you in years.

For who among us knows
how to swallow such a truth?

To know for certain
how many things we hoped were honesty
were, in fact, just whiskey.

That every song
we danced to that night was sung
by the Hallelujah Junkie Choir.

This boy
who always woke up smiling,

showed up at your door
with 3 tomatoes and a mango,
reached those dirty hands
into such dark things.

How humiliating.
And what does it say
about you?

Everything you still call love
he now calls Rock Bottom.

When the Boy from All the Old Poems
sends you a letter saying

I'm so proud of you,
and all the joy you have found
in the years that grew between us.

You will write back

I'm so proud of you too!
Look how clean we have become

in the hands of other people.

How lucky we are
to have realized love

Need look nothing
like a shot glass

or a shotgun.

Amy Winehouse Prays
to Her Own Funeral

They have been laughing for years,
but let this be my last,
best joke.

So funny, the way the cameras line the streets
to watch my hearse go by.

All of them looking like fork-toothed junkies
with their hands out, eyes big
like dinner plates.

Get it?

Because they all want the meat of me.
They want a smiling meal.

They never care about my sick. My lonely.
That's for me to swallow.

Isn't it great how we can all laugh
through the addiction?
Isn't this a fun game?

And I know, I'm sorry, I know,

Here at the end of the "joke"
There should be a punchline.

But all that's left is my dead body
is my father weeping
is my whole life gone.

And may you give them
the best joke.

May the whole word watch
and laugh,
and say nothing.

The Poet Stops the Book,
Climbs Off the Page,
and Speaks to You

I know, little star.
You want nothing of my joy.
You want the killing floor,
the meat hook,
the tidy slaughter.

So this is my knife.
I can carve whatever you want
from me.

Construct a God
out of my ruin.

I am here to be brave.

In Which I Stand
on an Oregon Beach at Sunset
and My Body Is Not a Ruined Church,
or a Man's Altar, or a Grave

And is instead just a girl's body
in August. The salt spit winter
of the Pacific Ocean,
swallowing up my knees.
Steam rising from my shoulders.
Alive Alive Alive.

Previously Appeared In

Early versions of "Explaining Girlhood to a Boy Who Has Never Been There" and "Girlhood, as I Remember" first appeared in *Voicemail Poems* as "Explaining Girlhood To A Boy Who Has Never Been There"

Early versions of "Sublimate," "Truism," and "Vigil" first appeared in *Drunk In A Midnight Choir* as "A Bad Weekend In Three Parts"

Acknowledgments

Thank you to my first readers: Samantha Peterson, Alex Dang, Brenna Twohy, Chris Leja, and my mom.

Thank you to Kiki Nicole and Lora Mathis for being the blood and bones of Where Are You Press. Thank you to Jamie Oliviera for the use of your beautiful illustration.

Thank you to EaT: An Oyster Bar for your $2.50 pilsners, without which this book would not have been written.

Thank you to my parents and grandparents, without whom this book would not have been possible.

Thank you to Alex, always, for being my home.

About the Author

Clementine von Radics

is a writer and the
founder of Where Are
You Press. As a spoken
word poet, she has
toured internationally
and across the United
States with Alex Dang
on *The Love and Whiskey
Tour*. This is her second
collection. She lives in
Portland, Oregon.

Also from Where Are You Press

This Is How We Find Each Other
Fortesa Latifi

Sullen Girl
Kiki Nicole

Give Me A God I Can Relate To
Blythe Baird

Healing Old Wounds With New Stiches
Meggie Royer

The Women Widowed To Themselves
Lora Mathis

It Looked A Lot Like Love
Kristina Haynes

Until I Learned What It Meant
Yena Sharma Purmasir

Are You Proud Of Me?
Alex Dang

Where Are You Press was founded in 2013. We
publish beautiful books of inspired, honest poetry by
women, people of color, and other marginalized
voices. We are based in Portland, Oregon.